MW00794925

FRAMES

a picture of death, drugs,

and forgiveness

as told to Amy Scheer

WITHDRAWN

KIRKENDALL PUBLIC LIBRARY
1210 NW Prairie Ridge Drive
Ankeny, IA 50023

Chapbook Press

Schuler Books
2660 28th Street SE
Grand Rapids, MI 49512
(616) 942-7330
www.schulerbooks.com

ISBN 13: 9781936243969
ISBN 10: 1936243962

Library of Congress Control Number: 2015938978

Copyright © 2015 Amy Scheer
All rights reserved.

No part of this book may be reproduced in any form without
express permission of the copyright holder.

Printed in the United States by Chapbook Press.

ADEL PARTE PUBLIC LIBRARY
1310 SW Prairie Ridge Drive
Ankeny, IA 50023

We sat down and Pat led us in the Lord's Prayer to start. Which was a very interesting experience for me because I grew up in this church where we did the Lord's Prayer every Sunday. We'd recite the words. And honestly, it was a chilling experience to say it in that moment. It was, you know, "Forgive us our trespasses as we forgive those who trespass against us." And I'm like, Holy crap.

OUR FATHER WHO ART IN HEAVEN,

HALLOWED BE THY NAME.

THY KINGDOM COME.

THY WILL BE DONE

ON EARTH, AS IT IS IN HEAVEN.

GIVE US THIS DAY OUR DAILY BREAD.

AND FORGIVE US OUR TRESPASSES,

AS WE FORGIVE THOSE WHO TRESPASS AGAINST US.

AND LEAD US NOT INTO TEMPTATION,

BUT DELIVER US FROM EVIL:

FOR THINE IS THE KINGDOM,

AND THE POWER, AND THE GLORY,

FOREVER.

AMEN.

She was coming down the tollway, and there were four or five cars in front of her that had come to a complete stop. The police say she was doing less than five miles an hour, if not completely stopped. And he came up from behind and never slowed down, never hit the brakes. He was doing about 80. They say between 80 and 88 was his speed.

The back of the car was pushed clear up to the front seat. To look at the car from the front wasn't bad, because she was pushed into the car in front of her. But the back, it was just no longer there. All of it was pushed up into the car. I've run the scenario many times of what if Trey would have been in the car. He clearly would have died.

Nobody sees how it was possible for me to actually be sleeping and go from the Winfield sign to the Farnsworth sign; that's about six miles, five or six miles. There was some hearsay that my car was seen kind of swerving, going excessively fast. I fell asleep and that sped up everything, just relaxing my foot on the gas pedal. In some of the pictures I've got, the gas pedal is bent. There's nothing wrong with the brake pedal; it doesn't show any indication the brakes were ever applied.

Marilyn had gone to visit her roommate from college, who had just had a baby. We debated: should we all go? I told her, "You go, focus on Jill and the baby. I'll stay home with Trey."

Trey and I had a pretty normal weekend until the police showed up at the door. A local policeman came to the door with a piece of paper. I could read it faster than he could talk. "Severe head trauma." For some reason, I had this overwhelming feeling that she had died. But they said call this number, call the hospital right away. The hospital I called, she hadn't even arrived yet, but the helicopter was landing. I hung up the phone and waited for them to call back. I was kind of working in panic mode. The officer said, "Do you want me to stay?" And I said, "Yeah."

I quick called good friends of mine, Derek and Joni, and they dropped everything and came over. Their knee-jerk reaction was that everything would be okay. "We'll help you with this; everything's going to be okay." They called Mike, the pastor of the church where I work, and they called some people to get together to pray.

I woke up. I was completely confused. I actually tried putting the airbags back, folding them up, and starting the car. I thought of the weed in the glove box and put it in my pocket. I was not wearing my seatbelt. The steering wheel was bent over from my ribcage. I heard all these people arguing, you know, "Don't touch him." "Wait for this, wait for that." "We gotta get him out."

And then I was yelling at the fireman, or whoever he was, because my shoes fell off as they pulled me out. I fell back asleep. I woke again, I was in the ambulance. They cut all my clothes off. They cut through the bag of weed. It fell down onto the floor. And a nurse was saying, "Oh, we gotta save this." That's when I blacked out again.

People immediately started gathering at the church. I had this back and forth dialogue with the hospital two or three times. They called me back, and it was the chaplain. I'm like, This is not good. I knew enough to know that if the chaplain's calling, it's not good.

The chaplain said, "We want you to know that Marilyn has arrived. They've been working on her. All we know is when they arrived on the scene, they needed to resuscitate her." They resuscitated her to a point where they could transfer her to another hospital.

He said, "We want you to know that it's very, very serious." I said, "I understand." I looked at Mike and Derek and Joni and said, "It's not good." Joni, bless her heart, said, "We have people praying." I love her to death but I was like, Don't tell me that everything's gonna be fine. You can't tell me that, because I know that it's not fine.

The doctor called back and said she had been non-responsive to pain stimulus since they found her. Because of that, she'd had no pain medication. They were only able to get a faint heartbeat in the field.

"I want you to start thinking if you want to use artificial means to keep her alive."

I panicked. This sounds terrible, but I thought, How's she going to be a mother? What's Trey going to do? You know, your mind just goes a hundred miles an hour.

The doctor said, "We're going to continue to work. We're doing a scan right now to see if there's any brain activity. If there is activity, the brain is still living, and we would put her on machines to breathe for her to keep her alive."

They called back within a minute and said, "We're terribly sorry; she's died."

THY WILL BE DONE

ON EARTH, AS IT IS IN HEAVEN.

I went back into the house and looked at my friends, and I just shook my head.

Joni said, "It's going to be all right."

And I said, "It's not, it's not."

I sat down on my steps. I had to tell them she was gone. Mike sat by me, and Derek and Joni, and nobody said anything. It was very, very quiet. We were all obviously crying, and kind of at a loss for anything. It felt like we sat there for a day and a half.

I sat there kind of staring, thinking, How am I going to do this? I really don't know if I have this in me to do what needs to be done. I just don't know.

Between the officer showing up at the door and us on our way to Chicago, hour and a half.

We rolled into Chicago in the wee hours of the morning. It was a very quiet ride. Mike and Derek didn't know what to say. I didn't know what to say back, so I just stared out the window.

In those early hours, the weirdest thing was this inner conflict of, I have to do this. I will do this. I need to be a dad. It's not going to be easy, but I need to pull myself up.

And then I would kind of flip a switch and think, No, I can't do this. I can't. I really can't. Inside my head, just going back and forth. And even all the way to Chicago, my mind kept flipping back and forth: I'm a good dad. I'm engaged in the life of my child. I change diapers. I know how to do laundry. I can do this stuff. But then, I don't want to do this. I don't care if I can, I don't want to. I'm not sure if I can.

The chaplain asked if I wanted to see her alone, or if I wanted him to be there. And I said, "I want to do it by myself." I remember walking down the hall to where this room was. He walked so slow. He was very quiet, calm—I think they're trained to be soothing. But I just kept thinking, Why are you so slow?

She was covered with a sheet from her neck down. She still had a neck brace on from the accident and looked very normal. I remember sitting there and not knowing what to do. Do you say *goodbye*? What do you do? I wasn't sure. I sat there for a while. I prayed.

I told her I was sorry that she had to deal with this. I was sorry that it happened and that this is where we were. Some time went by, and I sat there for a while thinking that at some point, I needed to leave the room.

I'm sitting here overlooking this beautiful valley, which I never would have believed existed if I weren't here. I'm alone at the top of the hill. Surrounded by yellow flowers I can't identify, I'm in awe of the creativity of God. I am comforted by the knowledge that God sustains even the frail, little plants.

Surely he'll take care of me.

I had to sign some papers to release the vehicle for investigation and the body for autopsy. There was a lot to get done; it was four in the morning and they're like, "Tomorrow you'll need to be in touch with us about a funeral home, etc.," and I was thinking to myself, You have no idea. There was something so strange about life being normal one minute, and less than twenty-four hours later sitting in a funeral home picking out a casket and discussing the quality of a vault.

I pulled up to my house: people everywhere. Marilyn's family is huge—all these brothers and sisters and their kids, and some of their kids that have kids. I did not live in a big house and there were thirty people there.

I met my brothers in the driveway. They don't hug, never saw them cry, but we did both.

About that time, upon my return, I realized that these people were all trying to honor Marilyn. I came to an appreciation for people willing to enter, the best they knew how, into what was going on. I kicked into this mode of being gracious to them because they had no idea what to say to me, and, quite frankly, I had no idea what to say to them. I thought, I'll be grateful for whatever they can muster up—if it's a hand on the shoulder or a pie, I'll accept that.

I learned over the weeks and months to come that I could have been offended on several occasions by people's inability to be a good friend, but I chose not to. I figured if I were them, I don't think I would have done any better. And that carried me a long ways. People have this really deep desire to make sense of what is happening around them, to feel like they have done something. The dynamic of working at the church really muddied that water—I don't necessarily know them all that well, but they know me.

The accident was Saturday, the funeral wasn't until the following Friday. I sat at home. There was nothing to do. We hadn't done visitation yet, so all these people were kind of chomping at the bit. I assigned somebody the job of answering the phone at my house, somebody the job of answering the door. I assigned the job of opening mail, because we couldn't keep up.

I took Trey to his room and sat down in the rocking chair with him. I realized I had to tell him his mom died. He knew something was different; kids know that stuff. I thought, I'm going to be the person that tells him. I don't want him to grow up and be ten years old and say, "Well, who told me, what was that like?" and not have an answer for him.

And so we sat in the chair and I told him. I explained that his mom was in an accident and that she loved him very much. I was crying as I told him this, and he knew that something wasn't right. He snuggled up to me and put his arms around me. And he was never like that. He was sixteen months old and always wanting to crawl and be on the move.

He just sat there and, in the way he could understand, he understood. I don't know exactly what that means. I don't know. I think as he continues to get older his understanding grows and keeps changing and developing as he develops. But in that moment, I knew he understood.

Later, as the weeks and months rolled on, he became more stressful. But in that moment, he was very comforting to me. He gave me a lot of hope and a lot of purpose, every day, just getting up and doing what needed to get done.

It was also comforting to me—though it came to bother me later—that he never really asked for his mom. He had never really said her name, so I didn't have to sit around and have him yell for Mom. I don't know if I would have been able to handle that.

I am so overwhelmed with love for Kevin & Treyton. As I reflect, I have difficulty grasping the grace that God has given me in such a healthy, happy baby and a strong, loving, tender, joyful husband. I feel like it's not enough to give you praise. Lord, what else can I give you?

We did it open. I could have gone either way, but the family on both sides said it was okay; it would be good for people to realize that wasn't her. Because of some of the complications post-accident, she did not look like herself at all. Lots of swelling, a lot of bruising. When I saw her at the hospital, it was nothing like that.

It was good in that the Marilyn we knew and loved was not the Marilyn that was laying there. People mentioned that to me. They're like, "You know, that really doesn't look like her and that's not how I'll remember her."

We started visitation at four o'clock. At ten o' clock, we were still there. The line was out the door the whole time. I stood there the whole time and talked to every single person because I wanted to. It was exhausting and very healing for me in a lot of ways—to see people who got in their car and drove hours, or got on a plane and flew was very, very moving.

These were people from different eras of her life: people who knew Marilyn as a child, in graduate school, at college, people who knew Marilyn before I did, people who knew us together and had moved away. These people had come through the line, all with a different slice of life they had shared with her, and they would share it with me. I learned more about her in five hours standing there—to hear person after person really praise her and who she was and the things that she had meant to them, and the reasons they were different because of her.

It wasn't a super sorrowful thing. We had had five days of crying; in a lot of ways, I felt like I didn't know how much more was in me. You know, you can have one of those guttural crying experiences, but you can't keep doing that. I just don't think it's in people to keep doing that.

PLEASE BE SEATED.

THE BIBLE TELLS US OUR HOPE IS IN THE NAME OF THE LORD, WHO MADE THE HEAVENS AND THE EARTH.

JESUS SAID, "COME TO ME. COME TO ME ALL YOU WHO ARE WEARY AND HEAVY BURDENED, AND I WILL GIVE YOU REST."

WE ARE HERE THIS AFTERNOON BECAUSE WE ARE WEARY. WE'RE HERE THIS AFTERNOON BECAUSE WE ARE BURDENED.

WE'RE HERE THIS AFTERNOON BECAUSE WE ALL LOVE MARILYN.

I INVITE YOU TO HEAR THE FAMILIAR WORDS OF THE TWENTY-THIRD PSALM. IT SAYS, "THE LORD IS MY SHEPHERD. I SHALL LACK NOTHING. HE LEADS ME BESIDE STILL WATERS, HE RESTORES MY SOUL. HE GUIDES ME IN PATHS OF RIGHTEOUSNESS FOR HIS NAME'S SAKE.

"AND EVEN THOUGH I WALK THROUGH THE VALLEY OF THE SHADOW OF DEATH, I FEAR NO EVIL. FOR YOU ARE WITH ME. YOUR ROD AND YOUR STAFF, THEY COMFORT ME. YOU PREPARE A TABLE FOR ME IN THE PRESENCE OF MY ENEMIES. YOU ANOINT MY HEAD WITH OIL; MY CUP OVERFLOWS. SURELY GOODNESS AND MERCY WILL FOLLOW ME ALL THE DAYS OF MY LIFE.

"AND I WILL DWELL IN THE HOUSE OF THE LORD, FOREVER."

Nighttime was the hardest for me. That's when I really missed her. I was busy enough during the day, but it got real quiet at night. Everything slowed down and my mind got to a point where I just missed her. It was hard for me to sleep alone.

You get so used to sleeping by somebody that I would take some of her clothes and put them in the bed, by a pillow or something, to kind of help me adjust. I thought to myself, This is crazy. You're crazy. I'm never going to tell anybody that I'm doing this because they're going to think I'm nuts.

I was thinking, Is this ever going to go away. Am I always going to feel like this?

IN THE MORNING WHEN I RISE

IN THE MORNING WHEN I RISE

IN THE MORNING, WHEN I RISE

GIVE ME JESUS

GIVE ME JESUS, GIVE ME JESUS

YOU CAN HAVE ALL THIS WORLD

GIVE ME JESUS

WHEN I COME TO DIE

YES, WHEN I COME TO DIE

WHEN I COME TO DIE

GIVE ME JESUS

GIVE ME JESUS, GIVE ME JESUS

YOU CAN HAVE ALL THIS WORLD

GIVE ME JESUS

FOR THE LIFE AND TESTIMONY OF MARILYN. FOR ALL THAT SHE WAS BY NATURE, AND BY GRACE,

>WE GIVE YOU THANKS, O LORD.

FOR HER LOVE AND COMMITMENT TO FAMILY. MOTHER OF TREY, WIFE OF KEVIN,

>WE GIVE YOU THANKS, O LORD.

FOR HER FRIENDSHIP THAT WAS GRACIOUSLY GIVEN TO OTHERS,

>WE GIVE YOU THANKS, O LORD.

FOR HER LOVE FOR CHRIST, HER PASSION FOR MINISTRY, HER MISSION TO THE WORLD,

>WE GIVE YOU THANKS, O LORD.

FOR JESUS CHRIST OUR LORD, WHO LOVES MARILYN, GAVE HIMSELF UP FOR HER. AND HAS PREPARED A PLACE FOR HER, WHICH SHE NOW ENJOYS IN HEAVEN,

>WE GIVE YOU THANKS, O LORD.

MAYBE YOU REMEMBER THE STORY OF LAZARUS. LAZARUS WAS A GOOD FRIEND OF JESUS.

BUT LAZARUS DIED. WHAT DID JESUS DO, WHEN LAZARUS DIED? JESUS, HE KNEW. JESUS KNEW ABOUT HEAVEN. JESUS, HE KNEW ABOUT LIFE EVERLASTING. JESUS, HE KNEW ABOUT NO MORE PAIN, HE KNEW ABOUT NO MORE TEARS, HE KNEW ABOUT NO MORE MOURNING, HE KNEW ABOUT NO MORE CRYING, HE KNEW ABOUT NO MORE WEEPING. OF ALL PEOPLE, JESUS KNEW. JESUS KNEW THAT LAZARUS WAS IN A BETTER PLACE.

SO WHAT IS IT THAT JESUS DID?

HE DIDN'T CELEBRATE. HE DIDN'T START DANCING WITH JOY. HE DIDN'T SAY, "NO, ALL THINGS WORK TOGETHER FOR GOOD TO THOSE WHO LOVE THE LORD AND ARE CALLED ACCORDING TO HIS PURPOSE." THAT'S NOT WHAT JESUS DID. WHAT DID JESUS DO?

THE BIBLE TELLS US THAT JESUS WEPT. JESUS GRIEVED.

GOD IS SAYING JESUS DID, AND SO CAN WE. IT'S OKAY.

GOD SAYS GRIEVE. BUT HE ADDS THIS ONE THING. HE SAYS, "GRIEVE WITH *HOPE*."

I was swimming. I found myself moving in and out of the gravity of it all. Sometimes I just felt numb: can't really cry anymore, not even sure this is real. Wondering if I just need to sleep and it will all be different the next day.

TO THE ALMIGHTY GOD, OUR HEAVENLY FATHER, WE COMMEND MARILYN LUPKES JANSMA. AND WE DO SO AS A PEOPLE OF HOPE. A PEOPLE WHO BELIEVE IN THE RESURRECTION. A PEOPLE WHO BELIEVE IN LIFE EVERLASTING. A PEOPLE WHO BELIEVE THAT JESUS WILL COME AGAIN. THAT HE WILL RETURN IN GLORY. AND THAT WHEN HE DOES, ALL WHO HAVE DIED WILL BE RAISED TO HIM, AND WILL BE MADE LIKE HIM. OUR FAITH IS IN THE LORD JESUS CHRIST, WHO IS ABLE TO BRING ALL THINGS, EVEN IN DEATH, TO HIMSELF.

MARILYN BELONGS TO JESUS. WE KNOW THAT AND WE BELIEVE THAT. HIS LOVE FOR HER, AND OUR LOVE FOR HER, WILL NEVER CEASE.

What I remember most about the service is leaving when it was done. I felt pretty good, like I held it together. I walked out, I was the first to walk out. I hit the threshold of the doors, and I walked out into the lobby area. And it hit me that I was alone. I'm all alone.

In my head, I know he'll provide. In my heart, I don't believe it will be what I want. I guess that's the rub. It will be what is best whether I like it or not.

The service was a blur, and then a new wave of sadness hit. All the pomp and circumstance was over, everyone was headed back to a normal life, and I was not. Would they go back to work or snuggle up with their loved ones that night and have a new appreciation for it all? I was jealous, but not angry at them. I wanted them to understand what they had.

Closure never came for me until a few months later. I was unsure what to "close" and what to open. I really didn't want closure; I wanted things the way they used to be. I wanted my wife back. Now that the funeral was over, I could start the journey to understand a new life.

I've learned that grief is unpredictable; God gives peace and strength beyond reason; and words express very little.

Each moment we enjoy life, someone else laments the loss of it.

Sometimes the struggle is the very agent we need to understand the joy of it all.

The tragedy in New York and my mom's death raised a lot of questions. Maybe God is not really in control. Maybe some things aren't significant enough for him to care about. But his eye is on the sparrow! Well, I've seen a lot of dead and broken-winged sparrows. Maybe things just slip out of his control?

I don't like these thoughts, because they contradict my most basic beliefs. But when my mom died, I found some comfort in believing that God didn't do this to me. I also found myself not only protecting myself from the loss but also from the shock. "If God knew, he would have prepared me for it."

That's when it hit me. Growing up, I knew my parents were older and that God could take them at any time. God did prepare me. He did know. I'm still working through this. Though this opens the door for some anger, I'm more at peace with the idea that God is in total control.

I would be driving down the road and just start crying for no reason. And I would think, What is this? I would get upset with myself, like, What is this all about? Knock it off. Like, I was on my way to do something and this is very inconvenient for me right now.

That went on for a season of time, where any little thing would trip the trigger emotionally to this response that felt very physical, like breathing. There's an emotional process, but there's a physical process, too.

The mom of a friend from high school sent me a card. And of the hundreds of cards that I got, this is the only one I remember. She had lost her husband in a tragic train and car accident thirty-four years earlier. She sent me this card and she wrote, "The best advice I can give you is to jump into the river of grief with both feet. Don't wait, and don't put a toe in, just jump right in." That was the card.

It was so true. I felt like those were words I needed to hear and I needed to take to heart.

"My aunt suffered a long time with cancer and died a very painful death. I'm so grateful that Marilyn didn't have to suffer." In their minds, finding a positive was their way of aligning themselves with me.

And I swear this happened: I had somebody say, "We had a precious family pet die, and we know what you're going through." No kidding.

I said something to the effect of *thank you* and walked away. I couldn't stand there anymore; it just drove me crazy. But in hindsight, I see that was the only tool they had to deal with me and their feelings. It's all they had.

Things started happening. I would get a call one day from somebody saying, "Hey, your mortgage has been taken care of this month."

I was gone for an hour or two, came back, and there was a freezer in my garage to put all the food in. We had nowhere to put the food, and somebody went and bought a deep freeze, put it in my garage.

Somebody dropped off a schedule, said, "Here's who's bringing your meals for the next two months." The church really did a good job, the best they knew how. The small group I was in saw themselves as the gatekeeper, and I'm glad. They buffered me, which was good.

"Dad," I said, "I need your help. I need to rearrange the furniture in my bedroom. I can't sleep in there—I need to turn the bed a different direction or something, it's too much the same. I think too much. All her stuff is there. I mean, everything."

And it was exactly how she left it. I'd go into the closet to get a shirt, and there was all her stuff, and it smelled like her. A constant reminder. And then I'd go to the shower and I'd have my bottle and her twelve bottles. I made some minor adjustments, small, for coping reasons. Like, I need to do some things or else I'm gonna go nuts. I'm gonna go crazy here. But there were certain things I didn't want to touch at all, I didn't want to change.

I couldn't move her clothes out of the closet. I couldn't take them out. The very things that were so hard for me, I couldn't do anything about. And so I found little things; I could move the bed. I didn't want to sleep in another room, but I couldn't sleep in that room. Everything was a conflict for me. I don't want it to change, but I know that sooner or later I have to change. Sooner or later, I have to move the shampoo.

The next chunk of time, I would talk to anybody about her death. I needed to process through it verbally. I don't know why—maybe it's just how I'm wired, but it was almost harder not to talk about it.

I started to go back to church. I'd go late, stand in the back, leave early, because I couldn't handle everybody asking how I was doing. I didn't know how to answer; I don't *know* how I'm doing. I feel good today, I feel bad. Part of me thought, Well, I think I'm doing okay, but I just lost my wife. So I'm really not okay. There's a big part of me that's not okay. But there's another part of me that is. So I'd just avoid them; if I didn't have to answer the question, that was better. I went in church, left. In and out.

After the funeral, Derek and Joni said, "Hey, if it's okay with you, we'd like to make Thursday a night that we come over and watch TV with you, have dinner, and hang out."

That was awesome. They were great friends and I looked forward to it. Marilyn and I always had a show that we watched together during the week, and this was their attempt at saying, Hey, let's take your mind off some of the things you don't get to do. Let's forge some new things.

So I started to kind of settle into the new way of doing things. And one of the hardest things was telling my parents to go home.

They had stayed a couple weeks after the funeral, and I finally understood that my parents couldn't stay forever; they were tremendously helpful, but I needed to either sink or swim. "I'm so thankful that you've been here," I said, "but you need to go. I need to figure out if I can do this on my own or not." It was very hard for me to say, and boy, was it hard on my mom. I'm not sure if she thought I could. I tried to put myself in her shoes; I knew this was hard for her. She cried a lot. She tried to convince me that she could come down more frequently. She worked part-time at a bank, and she's like, "I really don't need to work there, I could come down every other week and spend it here."

I said, "Mom, I have to do this. I have to learn how to do this on my own." I worried that I hurt her, but I knew I needed to do it. It was the right thing to do.

My parents left, and it was just Trey and me. I didn't have to go back to work—they wouldn't let me come back. That week was very difficult. It all started to sink in for me at that point. I wanted to stay home with Trey, but I needed to find a place for him to go when I went back to work. Marilyn and I had never talked about that; I didn't know what she wanted to do anymore. It became, like, This is my decision and it's all mine. Nobody's gonna make it for me.

I had to take over the responsibilities that Marilyn had done. I probably ruined a couple loads of laundry, you know. I had no purpose during the day other than being a parent. I would exhaust all my tricks by, like, eleven in the morning, and then would count the hours until he would take a nap. And there were days when he wouldn't take a nap. I'd put him in his room, and I'd lay down in front of the door while he played. I was so exhausted; I never snapped out of that. I'd think, Well, if he can't get out of the room he's safe, and that's the most important thing.

I didn't even feel like a dad. I started to be like, Okay, I'm either gonna lay on the floor in my son's room and cry about this, or I'm going to choose the other way. I've got to do something different. There was this separation within me; I had this ability to step aside somewhere in my mind and be able to look at myself and assess things. It's like I existed five feet above myself, and I could just look down and watch myself all day long. A conscious part of me was at work, but there was this very subconscious part of me that just had to keep grieving. That's when, inside me, things really started to happen.

THY WILL BE DONE

I had to come to grips with if this was God's plan. Did God do this?

I think Marilyn's death was sorrowful for him. But only God could have taken what happened to Marilyn and wove so many beautiful things out of it. The visitation, to have these people come through and share these experiences. Only God could do this.

In the weeks and months that followed losing Marilyn, I saw that I was not mad at God. I'm not sure why I never got mad. I certainly had many questions. How can I possibly live without Marilyn? How will I parent this small child alone? Questions, yes; anger, no. I have often wondered why some people get so angry with God when bad things happen, why people quickly shift the blame to God. I never got to that point. For some reason, I held on to the hope that God was on my side—crying with me, grieving with me, sad.

There was always a thread of hope that ran through my story. At times it was thin, almost unable to be seen, but it was always there.

Joni had had to call over to the prayer meeting and tell them Marilyn died. Imagine being in a room fervently praying the Lord's Prayer and having somebody walk in and say, "She didn't make it." It questions what you really believe about prayer and about God's ability to answer. Depending on where you're at, that can be a very troubling process to go through.

Can God protect us? Yes. Can God deliver us? Yes. He's in all of it.

After the accident, prayer seemed really pointless. What could I possibly say at this moment that's gonna change anything, or that's gonna make me feel any better about what has to happen next? Am I wanting him to be this ointment that makes me feel better? Is that really what I want the Creator of the universe to be?

That's how I had lived life before all this happened: I would pray more fervently when I was in trouble or felt like I needed something more. I'm careful not to do that so much now, but when I'm really honest, I admit I sound a little bit arrogant. I listen to myself, and it sounds like, I'm good enough, I'm smart enough, I put my mind to it, and with the power of God, I overcame. And I really dislike that. It rubs me the wrong way. Because I would like to believe there's something more to it than that; there's more to dealing with circumstances that happen in our lives than just choosing to wake up on the right side of the bed.

I could list a sheet full of names of people who would do better in a crisis than I would. I'm just like the majority of people who struggle to sit down and crack open their Bible and read it on a daily basis, and who feel like their prayer life is mostly inadequate. So I struggle with being seen as someone who has a strong faith, and then people thinking that's what I use as my crutch for how my life turned out. Or the reason this happens is because I'm this very good Christian.

What is a good Christian? What I think is remarkable about my story is that I'm not all that devout. I think, Okay, if Billy Graham were me, I would expect this kind of behavior out of him. He would turn to God, God would tangibly answer his prayers and divinely appoint a path for him that is clear and concise. The reason I feel that certain elements of my story are miraculous is because I am not that person. I am not that guy.

It's almost unfortunate that I work at a church. It casts a little shadow on the kind of person I am on the inside. I struggle just as much as the person that walks into the church on Sunday morning, who struggles to really follow who God is.

That's been a question mark for me. Did God choose to bless the process for me? Because I look at it and think, Only God could have taken me through those things in the way that he did. My natural inclination is to get even. I'm not spared from feelings of anger or resentment, or you name it. I'm a human being. And throw in extreme feelings of loss and grief and all that, my ability to be able to suppress those feelings becomes even more difficult.

Like the driver in the wreck. The driver. For a long time, that's what I called him. *Rick* is his name.

He called me the other day.

Right now he's doing weekend sentences where he's on house arrest during the week and he goes in on the weekends. I was surprised by his sentencing, what the justice system actually lets you do. That he can do house arrest during the day. But I'm okay with it.

He called me in late August on the third anniversary of the accident, and said, "I just wanted you to know I was thinking about you today, about the accident. I'm still sorry for what I've done, and I want you to know I've been clean since the day of the accident, for three years now."

People's reactions to him calling me were very interesting. Some of my friends still carry a lot of anger toward him. Like they've wrapped this whole thing up: He's the bad guy. "I can focus my energy there. He's the one I blame. I hold him responsible for what happened."

They're like, "What did you say to him? Did you yell at him? What did you do?"

I didn't say a lot. I told him I appreciated the phone call. You know, he didn't have to call me.

And they were like, "How do you know that he's really clean?"

I gave him the benefit of the doubt. If I was a user and I wasn't clean, I would avoid all contact. He can—I'm not calling or checking up on him, seeing how he's doing. I don't expect a report card from him.

I've been through something very difficult and tragic, but it was never my inclination to switch into that victim mentality of poor me, look what's happening to me. Part of that was where I am in life—Lord willing, I have a lot of life left; if I become a victim, I'm going to have a rough, long rest of my life. This is not gonna be any fun for me.

There are parts of me that have grown a little more cynical—I look at people and think, That's not suffering; get over yourself. And what's strange is I feel like I've grown in compassion at the same time. I've toughened up a lot more on the exterior, and I've grown far more tender than I ever was on the inside.

A friend of mine from church told me her friend's husband died in a plane accident. Her friend was thirty years old, had four kids at home and was pregnant with her fifth. Shelley asked if I would meet and talk with her right after it happened.

I said, "Absolutely, if she wants to, but I'll tell you right now that I don't have a list of advice to give her. If it's comforting for her to be with a person like me, I'd be more than happy to do that."

So we met. I identified a lot with her. But in the same breath, I could hold up a mirror to myself and think, Wow, you've changed a lot in the last three years. She'd say things and I'd be like, Oh my goodness, that is me. Like a glimpse at myself every once in a while. She had some unique struggles that I didn't have, but otherwise it was very real and very similar.

There was a strange amount of comfort that came from meeting with her, for me, and I hope I did some good for her. Sometimes you don't see things changing until you can kind of look back and compare it to something. Subconsciously, there have been changes going on.

Two, three months after Marilyn died, I would go to the store, look around and think, Everybody in the store is gonna die someday, and I'm not sure they know it. Because a couple of months before, I didn't know it. I looked at everything through the lens of *we're all gonna die someday*. Do these people have any idea that tomorrow, the very person they're with may not be here? Telling people became a burden. Like, Don't you all know? I could see how dying was just as important as living. How integral living was to dying. I had always compartmentalized the two: You're either living or you're dead. But those two roles don't exist without the other. And you can live in a way that affects how you die—not in the physical sense, but in every other sense.

This gave me a new perspective: Marilyn was never mine to own or to have. I shouldn't be upset that she's not here; I should be happy that I got what I got. And I really was—I wasn't just saying that to make myself feel better. I started to actually believe it. You know what? She was not mine. And Trey is not mine. We all belong to God.

My grandfather died in the 1980s, so Grandma's been widowed a long time. She and I were talking, and I found myself thinking about her being alone and widowed in her sixties. A lot of her social network had been dealing with it already. Her sister lost her husband. One of her best friends lost her husband. So there were people that came alongside of her and walked with her through that process.

For me, at twenty-six, death hit me like a train. I remember thinking later, Why don't they teach this in college? Everybody dies, but we don't teach classes on it. A lot of what I was taught, whether intentionally or unintentionally, was avoidance, or leveraging our belief system toward maximizing comfort. If you experience something difficult or something hard, well, pray more fervently.

I'd had several sessions with a counselor, a fabulous guy. We got on the subject of how I was feeling about the next season in my life.

He looked at me and said, "Has anybody ever told you that you did a good job?"

And I said, "What do you mean?"

He said, "At being married."

I said, "Well, yeah, Marilyn would say, 'You're a great husband.'"

He said, "No, that's not what I meant. Has anybody ever told you that you did exactly what God asked you to do in marriage, to love somebody until death? Has anybody ever looked at you and told you that you did exactly what God told you to do?"

I said, "No."

He said, "Well, let me give it to you. Everybody will come to the point where death will part them in their relationships on earth, and they will either complete that task or they will not complete that task. Kevin, you did everything God wanted you to do, and you did it really well."

At that moment, I was liberated. I became okay with being single. I didn't see myself as the wounded widower as much as I saw myself as someone who was faithful and honest. I shifted how I thought about myself. It was like there was a newfound purpose and fire that was lit in me again. I can be a single dad. I can do a good job of this.

It was about that time I met Kelly.

From: "Dr. Kelly Van Haaften"

Subject: RE: a not-so-quick note

Date: December 2, 2004 9:34:37 PM CST

To: "Kevin Jansma"

Hi KJ

How has your week been? Did you and Trey have a
nice Thanksgiving with family and/or friends? I have
been keeping you in my prayers, especially during the
upcoming holiday season. Be sure to let me know if
there's any way I can be helpful… the offer still stands
for free babysitting anytime you need it! Sometimes it's
nice to spend time with kids when I'm not struggling to
put drops in their eyes. ☺

Blessings,

Kelly

A few months after the funeral, I was giving a sermon at church and I noticed Kelly. I went up to her, and she was surprised I remembered her from college.

I said, "You visiting?" And she was like, "No, I've been going to church here for three, four months."

We started talking about ministry things. A friendship. We talked on the phone after I put Trey to bed. Then we got to the point where we thought we should probably have a talk about what's going on here. Neither of us knew.

Is this okay? Is this legal? I started having feelings for Kelly, but on the inside, I still loved Marilyn. I knew I could do both because I was. Here I am, I still really love this person that I spent all this time with and had a child with, and now I've got something else going on here. And this one's not disappearing at all. How in the world do I tell people that?

From: "Dr. Kelly Van Haaften"

Subject: RE: Thanks

Date: December 15, 2004 11:18:09 AM CST

To: "Kevin Jansma"

KJ -

Right back at ya! I am so thankful for your friendship and the ways that I have been able to get connected at the church – it makes me feel like I am at home there.

You know, I was a very different person during my college days... I'm not sure if you would have ever wanted to hang out back then! ☺ I can definitely say that I have matured and mellowed a bit over the years.

I hope you have a great week!

~Kelly

p.s. How was Ocean's 12? I've heard mixed reviews...

I remember the first time she came over to my house for dinner. Trey was there. We were both in the kitchen doing something, and I remember Trey being protective. He would always want to stand between her and me, hold onto my leg, like, Leave my dad alone.

When you've got a small child at home, you don't just date for fun. I didn't want to drag my child through that, so we worked at dating under the radar. Kelly didn't want the scarlet letter; we both kind of had our own fears about the relationship. But there was something strong enough that made us want to keep trying.

From: "Dr. Kelly Van Haaften"

Subject: RE: you make me laugh

Date: January 4, 2005 10:29:23 PM CST

To: "Kevin Jansma"

KJ –

No, I do not look at you and think your life is a complicated mess. I mean, we all have our complications… maybe some people's are just more visible than others… and I have my share of complications too and that topic we will just save for another time.

Next topic – what it is like sitting on my side of the table. Well, you know, when I think about it, I just always have a great time with lots of laughs when we talk or get together – and in some ways it's just as simple as that. But honestly, at first I was a little nervous even when I talked to you at church for the first time. Okay, a lot nervous. I wasn't sure how to express the sympathy I was feeling for you, and I have never really been close to anyone who has gone through the grief that I knew you were dealing with. I guess I never thought that we would even be able to reconnect... basically, I didn't want to intrude on your life because I knew that you already had a tight circle of friends and people from the church who were supporting you. Does that make sense?

It's funny that you say you are surprised by my level of reciprocation because I have been just as surprised that you have been interested in letting me into your circle and maybe even "complicating" your life more than it already is?!?!?!??! ☺

Now it's time for my honest confessions. The hardest thing that I have been struggling with lately is feeling like I am getting too over-excited about our relationship... like letting my mind get a little carried away with where things could lead in the future. Do you know what I mean? I am really praying that God will help me to just take it day by day. I mean, as a single woman in my upper 20s, I know that I am not getting any younger each year and like anyone else, I want to meet that person that God has picked out for me but I also have come to realize that it won't be according to my timeline, and I am learning to just be patient and wait for God's perfect timing.

Besides all that, I am very interested in getting to know you better, and I think we have a great friendship started here. I don't think that we necessarily have to define it as "dating" or whatever.

It's all good,

Kelly

p.s. and now I am trying to decide whether to go to bed or wait up for a response email?!?

From: "Kevin Jansma"

Subject: RE: you make me laugh

Date: January 4, 2005 10:51 PM CST

To: "Dr. Kelly Van Haaften"

I have to tell you- I have been ready for bed for about an hour- I just sat through the entire Amber Frey interview on Dateline- hoping that you would write back tonight- Amazing how people take a long time to write back when every few minutes you look at your screen to see if your in-box is flashing. I do feel like a loooooooooser☺☺☺☺☺☺

Anyway- you have no idea how good it is to hear your thoughts on everything- I agree that as long as this whole thing is God led we have no worries, but I also agree that there is no hurry to define things yet other than perhaps "budding friendship"☺☺ I have spent many nights thinking and praying about the timing of our newfound friendship. I 100% feel like it has developed out of pure motives and intentions, and I want you to know my intention is to just keep getting to know you. When I boil things down to their simplest form, I am very interested in getting to know you better.

But I am also not in any hurry to move into a relationship too quickly. I am OK being alone, but I choose not to be if the timing is right, and the other person (like you☺) is OK with that, does that make sense? I feel like a dork even writing some of this stuff. I feel like I am in high school again in a way.

I think it is very funny to hear what you thought about meeting me for the first time at church. I may not show it, but I was the nervous one. I remember feeling a bit nervous, but for some reason it just felt really good to see you that day. In response to your thoughts of me not having room in my circle of friends… as you can see by the sheer amount of time I have open to e-mail- my circle has room for more☺

Have a great nights sleep!

kj

I had worked really hard at grieving, but not everybody around me had. I was scared to death to tell them I was thinking about asking a woman on a date, because I didn't think they would approve. And their friendships were very important to me. They were key to me, it was where I was at.

People would talk about Marilyn in a flattering but kind of fabricated way. I don't think it was intentionally dishonest; I think some of it was their way of immortalizing her. But some things would make me very uncomfortable. It was almost like people would test me to see if I had forgotten about Marilyn or had replaced her.

Once, someone implied that Marilyn was no longer a part of my life. I was very careful to tell them that even though I was seeing Kelly, I still loved Marilyn and the relationship we had.

When I was back working at the church and Kelly and I were dating, she would often pick up Trey from the nursery when I was busy. She would bring him to where I was and maybe we'd go have dinner together or something, or she would take him during another service while I was at church. And the walk down the hall in church for Kelly was almost like the walk of shame, in that everybody was watching her.

She's a strong woman. There are people who couldn't have handled that.

Everything in me wanted to say, "My wife died. She's not my mistress; we're dating." I fought those feelings all the time. And what was even harder was there was a part of my subconscious that knew the majority of people weren't looking at me like that. But I still felt that way.

Our engagement was a turning point. People knew we were serious about the relationship—maybe it put them at ease that we weren't going to hurt each other with something that wasn't going to work out. It was a bit of a weight that was lifted for us both. We could plan, move forward, and it all felt more legitimate and real.

Between dating and the wedding was a year and a half, including the engagement. It wasn't all that long, the time frame. When we first got engaged, my mom seemed to be having a hard time. I pinned her down one day and said, "Are you having a hard time with all of this? Are you okay with what's going on here?"

"Oh yeah, I'm fine. I'm fine."

And I said, "No, Mom, really, I'm not getting that vibe. I'm really not."

I pushed because I could. I said, "What's bothering you?"

Finally she cracked and said, "What am I supposed to do with your and Marilyn's wedding picture?"

I said, "What do you mean?"

She said, "When you and Kelly get married, what am I supposed to do with your and Marilyn's wedding picture?"

She's got all the boys' wedding pictures on the mantel in the living room. I looked at her and I said, "Leave it up."

She gave me a look. I said, "Mom, I'm really proud of the marriage I had with Marilyn. And I'm proud of the relationship I have with Kelly just as much. It's okay if you want to leave it up. Just don't put one in front of the other."

I needed Kelly in my life. I had convinced myself that I would do okay and be all right. I'm glad I had, but there are aspects she brings into our house and our family that I cannot. Not like decorating and cleaning—there's an element of nurture that I didn't know I didn't possess. There was something about the day that Trey stopped calling my name all the time and started calling hers.

It's strange for me to think that Kelly has been with Trey twice as long as Marilyn ever was. Kelly knows Trey. In a lot of ways I'm really grateful that Trey hadn't been six and that we'd have years and years of rethinking and helping make sense of it. It was pretty seamless for him.

I'm not gonna lie and say that it's always easy—there have been some very challenging times for us, and probably more for Kelly than anybody. She just wants to be normal like everybody else, and we are very normal people. I think sometimes there's this little bit of false celebrity that surrounds our life, like, "Oh, they're such a miracle." And we are, but, you know, we argue about the toilet seat, too.

I look at the Marilyn era, and I look at the Kelly era, and I compartmentalize them a little bit. Each one of them has its shining moments. Each one of them has its own challenges, frustrations, and difficulties. And it's not like Kelly is married to the same guy Marilyn was married to. I'm so profoundly different because of that part of my life. The whole soul mate mentality bothers me. I'm the opposite, the black eye of that theory. People will say things that don't fit into how I believe anymore. Like, "Isn't it great that they look down on you from heaven." And nobody's ever said this one yet, and I'm waiting for it—it'll probably come later in life—that Marilyn's death was God's reason for me to meet Kelly. I'm kind of waiting for that—I'm sure somebody will say it.

Because I don't think that God's plan was for Marilyn to die tragically in an accident so I could meet Kelly. But do I think it was part of God's plan for me to meet Kelly? Yes. So what do I do with that? I don't fret about it, but I sure as heck don't know how to explain it to people.

When Kevin and I first started spending time together, there were many framed pictures up around his house of Marilyn with her friends and of Marilyn with Kevin and Trey. I encouraged Kevin to keep them up, because the pictures symbolized that it was okay to think about Marilyn and talk about her. A lot of people wondered about that, especially with me around. So I felt if the pictures were still up on display, it was a way to show others that her memory was still a part of our conversation and wasn't something that we were trying to hide or forget.

When we were dating, I helped Kevin choose a nice matte and frame for a special photo of Marilyn and Trey taken just before she died. We framed the photo and had it prominently displayed in Trey's bedroom. Over time, and when Kevin moved out of his old house, many of the other framed photos were taken down and carefully boxed up for storage. My sense of decorating is different than Marilyn's in that I don't have a lot of framed pictures on my walls, just a few special ones. But that framed picture of Marilyn has always remained in Trey's room. It was very important to both Kevin and me that Trey would grow up

knowing that he has two mommies. We
wanted to keep the pictures up as a way
for him to remember her face and know
that it was okay to ask questions about
his mommy in heaven.

Trey used to call Kelly "New Mommy." He was three at the wedding. He knows he has a mom in heaven and a mom here on earth. That God gave him one mommy for just a little while.

Trey's gonna grow up, you know. As Kevin put it, he has a mother here, and he has a mother in heaven. That really got to me. It really did.

Kevin wanted to meet with me.

ON EARTH, AS IT IS IN HEAVEN.

GIVE US THIS DAY OUR DAILY BREAD.

To me, Rick looked like someone who did drugs. He didn't look healthy. He looked probably five, six years older than he really is. His wife worked at an office, really seemed to have her act together. Pat had said she was not a user, never was.

His wife's name was Kelly.

We sat down and Pat, the moderator, led us in the Lord's Prayer to start. And honestly, it was a chilling experience to say it in that moment. It was, you know, "Forgive us our trespasses as we forgive those who trespass against us." And I'm like, Holy crap.

Kevin read me a letter. I didn't write a letter. Writing an essay for school is one thing; preparing yourself to tell someone your feelings, you'd alter it so it sounds good. So I showed up there basically with nothing, and my wife came with.

"Never in a million years would I have thought that I would end up here. Sitting in a meeting of this nature. But here I am. And here you are. I have had a couple of years to formulate my thoughts about what I would say to you. To be honest, it is hard to know where to start, so I guess the beginning, or at least the beginning of how our lives intersected, is a good place to start: August, 2004.

"I got a knock at the door. I opened the door expecting to see a friend, or someone selling something, but instead I saw a police officer. I could see by the expression on his face that all was not good. 'Sir, your wife has been in a very bad accident, she has suffered massive trauma to her head.' I immediately couldn't breathe. It was like I got punched in the gut. At that moment the thought flashed through my mind: She is dead. Marilyn is dead. Within twenty minutes of being on the phone with the ER doctor, my worst nightmare was confirmed.

"As I stood in shock over what was happening, I looked across the room at Trey. He was toddling around the room making noise and saying one of his three or four words that he knew, and he had no idea what was happening."

Rick immediately started crying, and his wife did, too. The letter was probably seven pages typed, and I'm reading and they're crying. They're in tears the whole time. To his credit, he made eye contact with me the whole time. And I really respected that.

I broke down pretty bad. It also got my wife. With my wife sitting next to me, nobody sitting next to Kevin, that really brought out, you know, if somebody took her from me, I don't know what I would do. Don't know what I would do.

"We arrived at the hospital about 1:00 a.m., and Marilyn's friend Jill and her husband were waiting for us. They had been there all evening. I was comforted by the fact that they had been with Marilyn. I was glad she didn't need to be alone.

"The first person that talked to me was the chaplain. He walked me through some paperwork that I needed to sign. He then introduced me to a state trooper.

"The trooper informed me that the accident was under investigation, and that I needed to give permission for Marilyn's car to be impounded for crime scene reconstruction. I was a little shocked and confused, but I agreed. He went on to tell me that there was some question as to the driver of the car that hit Marilyn and what was going on, as they found some evidence of drug use in the car. I didn't know what to do with this new information. It didn't surprise me, but it didn't change the fact that I was here to see my dead wife. Nothing they could tell me would bring her back.

"The chaplain led me down a long hallway and into a room that Marilyn was in. I was given some time alone with her. I sat by her side and thought about heaven. What it must be like. How Marilyn was there in that very moment.

I cried, prayed, and sat. I could not believe I was sitting in a room with my dead wife."

There were so many thoughts and feelings I needed to lay on the table for this guy. If anything, just to broaden his understanding of his actions. I really wanted Rick to understand the scope of how he changed my life, because I felt like he was pretty disconnected from it, to a certain extent. He understood the obvious, like, I killed this guy's wife. But I don't think he understood all the other stuff, like how I cried many nights because of complications with insurance; it was horrendous.

And I was probably sadder for Trey than I was for myself a lot of days. Most of my anguish was when I was with him. Here's a small child that doesn't have a mom. What a rip-off. What a rip-off.

"She was a loyal friend. She cared deeply about those less fortunate than her. She was a fantastic wife. She was a great mother. She would have done anything for Trey. So many people were touched by the legacy she left. Even at the young age of twenty-nine."

AND FORGIVE US OUR TRESPASSES,

AS WE FORGIVE THOSE WHO TRESPASS AGAINST US.

AND LEAD US NOT INTO TEMPTATION,

BUT DELIVER US FROM EVIL:

"Over the past two years I have thought of you often. I have wondered what you were doing. And I have wondered what really happened that day, if you feel bad about the accident. If you have changed your life. If you still use drugs and alcohol. I have wondered what kind of punishment you have had to endure, and if you are really sorry for the lives that you have changed. Have you moved on with your life? How have you changed?

"People have asked me if I am mad at you, if I want to sue you or anything like that, and I tell them no. I can truthfully look you in the eye today and tell you I am not mad at you. I know there is nothing that you can do to make things better. You cannot bring Marilyn back to life. Ultimately, I cannot judge you for what happened that day. It is not my job. I believe that someday God will judge you. He knows your heart and how you feel. And someday you will stand before him and need to be accountable for your actions, just like I will.

"Choosing not to be angry at you does not mean that I think you should not be punished. I think that you should be accountable for your actions, but it is not my job to do that.

"I believe that God offers us all forgiveness. No matter what we have done. Despite the pain you have caused me in my life, I believe that you can be forgiven for your actions.

"Despite the challenge and difficulty that I have faced in the past two years, I feel that God has been the only thing in my life that has allowed this unfortunate event to grow and change me for the better instead of destroy and fill me with bitterness. I wanted to meet with you today to help you understand that. I hope that you can change your life. I hope that you can find space in your heart for God's unconditional love.

"I forgive you for the things that have come from your actions in my life. I hope that you will change your life. I pray that you will choose to turn from the behaviors that contributed to the events that took place that day in August two years ago."

"I don't hate you. I forgive you."

Pat said, "Okay, now you have a chance to say what you'd like to say." He sat and he thought.

He said, "First of all, if you had done to me what I've done to you, I don't think I'd ever forgive you. If someone took my wife away from me in that way, I'm not sure I could do that."

It took a lot of visits to the shrink, a lot of visits, for me to understand why it was acceptable for him to forgive me.

And he said something like, "I can't tell you exactly if I fell asleep, if I passed out, but what I want you to know is that my lifestyle killed your wife."

I didn't go into that meeting looking for an apology, but him owning up was very healing for me. Instead of having everybody else in the world tell me that it was this guy's fault, to have him say, "My choices caused your wife to die," it was almost like a weight was lifted. There was healing power in just hearing him say it and be accountable for his actions.

I would have to say the very first time I started smoking pot was around twelve, about twelve. I moved down to Tennessee when I was twelve, for about a year and a half. I don't know if I want to blame it or not, but there was a point of time between twelve and about thirteen-and-a-half, almost fourteen, that little two-year section, when some situations happened, that I was abused. And by being sexually abused and then, also, the guy that did it saying, "Hey, come down and smoke some pot," yada, yada, yada—my mother thinks that's the reason why. Obviously, if my father was keeping a better eye on me, you know, I wouldn't be going down to the neighbor's house getting abused and smoking pot. And I was eventually drinking, following with the same person.

Shortly after that, at about fourteen, I came back up north here with my mother. I had the smoking pot trend going on which never really ended. Fifteen, sixteen, started getting friends with licenses and cars; sixteen, had my own car. And by then I was probably an average pot smoker—you know, three, four times a day.

Once I turned seventeen, the crowd I continued hanging out with started to do coke. I got a part-time job in a gas station, it was midnights, and doing coke all night kept you up. So that's when I started that. Reaching twenty, I ended up stopping. I did still smoke pot—not as much, of course, because I'm working. You smoke when you get home, relax, that kind of thing. I was doing it a couple of times, maybe once a day.

But then I really started getting into cocaine again. Went beyond regular, just sniffing coke to free-basing it. I did that up until August 21, 2004, my twenty-first birthday. My golden birthday.

It was a Friday night, and a bunch of friends and I went out. We wanted to celebrate my golden birthday the next day—you know, twenty-first of August, turning twenty-one, everybody thought it had to be twice as big. Went out drinking, stayed up 'til about three, three thirty. We did pot, we did some coke.

A way of coming down from coke, of course, is smoking pot. I didn't finish all the pot I had. I put it in the glove box of my truck. Went home, got a couple hours of sleep, had to be at the dealership at six-thirty. And you know, I was tired. A couple of times at work, during the middle of the day when we were slow, I would go outside and kind of doze off. I knew I was way, way tired. And then toward the end of the day it's like you get your second wind. Okay. I can make it home.

The last thing I remember was I see the Winfield sign and I always get off at 59. I remember putting my arm down, like resting my elbow on the ledge, just before the window. That's the very last thing I remember—the Winfield sign, doing that, and I woke up at the exit of Farnsworth in the ditch.

I owe Kevin my life for many reasons. I took a life from him. If Kevin asked me to do anything, I wouldn't hesitate. It was all up to Kevin whether or not I'm here now. If the prosecution and the family wanted to hammer down on me, they could have hammered down on me.

In the accident, I had hit my head quite hard. There was blood around my heart, my liver was bruised, nothing that couldn't be fixed. I was able to heal; unfortunately, other people weren't. I wasn't nearly as hurt as what I deserved. I'm one to say sometimes, There's an eye for an eye. And then, other times, it's just like, Well, maybe there's not. I didn't go on being stupid, I didn't go on doing drugs. If that were me looking at somebody doing that, then I would say, "Hey, you know what? Maybe you should have died. Maybe it should have been an eye for an eye."

There was a lot of doctors that said, "You weren't wearing your seatbelt, your heart's damaged." They called my wife and said there was a possibility of heart surgery. At one point, I thought, This is it: I'm getting punished for all the stupid stuff I've done, and you know, the list is long.

But God let me live, I think to help somebody. I got so many people come in right now, they're sitting there counting their dollars, how much they have. I say, "You know what? You don't have much money, let's just look at your car and see what's wrong with it." This guy coming from down the street with a $400 estimate, I fixed his car for $160. Just take care of people, do whatever I can.

Another part of that is doing something to change my life, how corrupt I was in school. I enjoy cooking, so in the past month and a half, my wife's convinced me to sign up for cooking school, so I'm going to go back to school. I think it will change my attitude if I learn the discipline, for one, that culinary arts will teach you. Doing what I love to do. And then, maybe I'll make a great restaurant that thousands of people will love.

Everything that I can do, I'm doing, down to the littlest things for an employee. It's not that it's gonna fix it, but that's what I'm doing. I used to be very negative, think of the glass as half empty. My wife's changed me into seeing the glass is half full. That's the way I'm trying to look at things.

I'll never forget the accident, and neither will Kevin. I had dreams probably for about three to four weeks. Those weird dreams that don't make sense at all. You wake upside down and then you flip back up—just weird, you know. But the drug dreams, I would say, they probably stopped maybe a year ago. Not that long ago.

Ether is used here in the shop. Ether is a real flammable liquid; it's also what they put in cocaine. The only aroma that cocaine has is ether. I can walk back in the shop and know immediately they have been using ether, and it will make my heart race a little bit. Do I get a craving to do it at that time? No. But it's just like, I don't even want to come back here. It's kind of a trigger, but not a trigger to say, I'm going to pick up some coke. I've finally gotten way beyond that.

There's all kinds of reminders. Everything makes me think of it. We had an older lady hit the wall. She pulled in and hit the gas instead of the brake, hit the wall of the car wash. A loud bang and then she was a little bit unconscious. She left her foot on the gas, so she just spun the tires, and smoke started coming up from the car. Something like that spooks me, gets me back into thinking. I get flashbacks. But it's not my trigger to start getting depressed and think about drugs—that's my trigger to help somebody. I ran to where this lady was. She wanted to get out, her husband wanted to help her. I talked the husband out of pulling her out. I called the ambulance right there. I wanted to make sure she was okay.

ACKNOWLEDGMENTS

I had been writing profiles for Northwestern College when, in June of 2007, the request came to interview alumni Kevin Jansma. Two memories from that time: first, it almost didn't happen—I had started another job and tried to pass on the story—and second, during the interview, Kevin mentioned meeting Rick almost in passing, as if forgiving the man who killed your wife was no big thing. He almost didn't want to talk about it.

So thank you, Duane Beeson, for insisting I meet Kevin. And thanks, Kevin, for telling me your story back then, and for entrusting it in my care over the many years since. I felt a weighty burden to present this narrative in a format fitting its complexity, which, by nature, asked for more than a fair share of raw truth. Kevin, you've been vulnerable throughout this process, and I am grateful for the bonds that connect us. We followed an inner leading to complete this project, and all the way you gave so much of yourself, not knowing what this stranger might make of your story. I thank you for trusting me.

Kelly, you surprised me with your candor. To weep openly over your husband's loss shows a deep personal strength; had this story been fiction, your strong character would hardly have been believed.

Jill, you welcomed me into your home and gave me the gift of your time and private thoughts. Though they don't appear in this book, please know that the spirit of our conversation helped shape the book's direction.

Kim, you steered me with a solid hand and preserved the heart of the book. Lori, you were an early, discerning reader, and I appreciated the insider advice. Rachel, you polished the final product with such professionalism; I am so grateful.

Cheerleaders Krista and Eric, thank you. Staff of 826Michigan, your Great Write-Off pushed this book toward completion; Dave Eggers's postcard hung above my desk, urging me on. Charlotte, what would we have done without your fast fingers? Thanks for transcribing the dozens of hours of interviews.

Greg, you have always made a path for my projects, with a love and support I can barely repay. Thank you for always honoring my work, and for clearing things with the extended family, who graciously released me from Thanksgiving weekend festivities for the past too many years. I love you and our little big boys, my most astute readers.

Thank you, Rick. I think of you often.

My privileged look into Marilyn's journals showed me the thinking, passionate person she was. Thank you, Marilyn, for your guiding light. It was very difficult to watch your journal pages go blank in late June of 2004; I am comforted only in believing that your last request, to rest in your Savior's arms, came to you sooner than you could have known.

Amy Scheer

December 2013

AFTERWORD

As we near the tenth anniversary of Marilyn's death, I find it difficult to grasp all the ways my life has changed since then. My three-year-old son Anderson is playing next to my chair as I write this. He has no understanding of who Marilyn was or that his older brother came from a different mom; he only knows that he is loved. Looking at him reminds me of the great power God has to heal us, provide for us, and work things out for good.

My memories are as vivid today as they were when I recorded them for this book, but there is less sting now. I don't know that time heals all wounds, but I can say that time, in my case, has allowed for a new perspective: gratefulness for God's hand in my life, and for the new beginnings and adventures that grew out of some very dark days. I am also reminded that my story is mine alone, while others will have a different interpretation of the events that happened. In the end, that's okay; we are all on our own journeys.

I view love and loss differently now. I no longer carry around a deep sense of worry or burden, because I know that so much of life is temporary. We can hold things, but we can't hold them too tightly. Loss is part of our world, and the love we have for each other is the great glue holding it all together.

Life is surprisingly normal. Kelly's companionship has been the greatest gift to me; I am grateful that the heart has the capacity not only to love once, but to grow again in love. I have moments, especially if she's traveling, when I catch myself wondering what I would do if something happened to her. It makes me afraid that I couldn't handle losing someone I love again. I quickly remind myself that fear can't drive us, but at the same time, I'm glad I can't imagine life without her. What a great testament to God's faithfulness in bringing us together.

Kelly adopted Trey on June 19, 2007. From time to time, we look at his baby book and talk about his mom in heaven, but his memory bank and life experience is with Kelly and our current family. Marilyn would have been proud of him. He's a great kid, and I am grateful that he does so well despite having lost his mother at a young age. When I think of Marilyn, it is always in relation to Trey. She would have loved seeing him grow up.

I still think about Rick. I don't have any unfinished business with him, but deep down I want to see his life changed, long term, for the good.

This project, like my story, is also an example of God's provision. Amy Scheer didn't know me at all when we first talked on the phone for a short article in my college's magazine, but her interest in my life turned into a new friendship and a great admiration for someone who was once a complete stranger. I remember sitting across the table from Amy for hours telling her about Marilyn's death. I looked up to see tears in her eyes, as she was totally engaged in my life story. Amy has invested countless hours of time and emotional energy, and I am grateful for her creativity and her heart for communicating my story. I am no writer, and this book is only possible because of her.

I am also grateful to my good friend Adam Clarke for his support and friendship. We have weathered many of life's storms together, and having his help on this book is very meaningful to me.

When so much darkness exists in the word, standing where I am today is a testimony to a loving God who cares deeply for us and has surprising things in store. For all of this, I am grateful.

Kevin Jansma

Thanksgiving 2013

"Do not be anxious about anything, but in everything, by prayer and petition, with thanksgiving, present your requests to God. And the peace of God, which transcends all understanding, will guard your hearts and your minds in Christ Jesus."

Phil 4:6-7

In memory of Marilyn Lupkes Jansma

1975—2004

FOR THINE IS THE KINGDOM,

AND THE POWER, AND THE GLORY,

FOREVER.

AMEN.